# SAP NAVIGATION GUIDE

# &

# COMMON COMPONENTS

## YOGI KALRA

ISBN: 10: 1977850197

ISBN-13: 978-1977850195

# TABLE OF CONTENTS

# FOREWORD

One of the primary learning curves in SAP is navigation. Often SAP has been criticized for being very frustrating to learn as the screens seem complex and very intimidating. Every new SAP implementation invariably has training courses only for navigation and basic guidance. Mastering navigation in SAP is half the battle won. This book has attempted to remove the phobia around this navigation by walking you though the basics and making the learning curve easier and less complex. Use F1 for help liberally – it will help you wade through the screens understanding everything thoroughly. As is the case with all seemingly multifaceted structures, the base of SAP is very simple. In spite of SAP's complexity as an ERP system, its edifice is built on very easy processes as you will notice while going through this book. Processes that are uniform, scalable and easily comprehensible.

Also included in this book are some chapters which occasionally make up a different section or even books in their own right – like variants and queries and since they are typically common across entire SAP, I have included them for the sake of learning as knowledge thereof makes day to day life in SAP very smooth and stress-free.

Your inputs and criticism are very welcome. If there is anything the author can do to help you understand the subject better or guide you in any way, please feel free to drop an email to shefariaentinc@gmail.com noting the name of the book in the subject of the email. Obviously there will be some errors and omissions in the book. I will be very grateful for your comments and responses if you find them or even otherwise since they will work to make the next edition better.

# SAP SYSTEM ARCHITECTURE

Generally, in the SAP environment, a three-system landscape is the norm though the complexity of this landscape will really depend on how simplified or elaborate the SAP system itself is at the company. The 3 tiers in the system landscape consists of Development Server (Dev), Quality Assurance server (QAS) and Production Server (PROD).

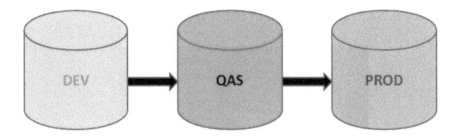

*Figure 1*

First all the development objects are completed in development system and then transported to the quality system where functional testing of business process are performed. Ultimately, they are transported to the production system which is the live system for end users and contains all the latest true business data.

Any correction or changes will also first be made in the development system and then changes shall be locked in a Transport request (Also known as TR number) then changes are moved to subsequent systems for testing and finally imported in production system (Live Business System).

This is not to be confused with the R/3 suffix of SAP. R/3 – 'R' signifies Real time and 3 means 3 tiered structure, these tiers being database server, the application (programs) server and the client (aka SAP GUI). This book will explain a lot more about this GUI (Graphical user interface) as we go along.

## SAP LOGON

To access SAP, double click in the SAP logon PAD.

*Figure 1*

You are shown a list of servers that you could log into; right now there is only one server as below. Each server points to an independent SAP system which has a database and a program server.

*Figure 2*

You are shown a list of servers that you could log into; right now there is only one server as below. Each server points to an independent SAP system which has a database and a program server.

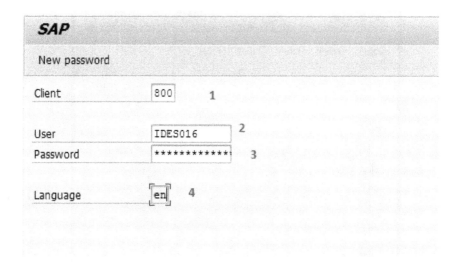

*Figure 3*

1. **Client:** A client is used in SAP system for multiple login on single instance. You can create multiple clients on a single instance. It also provides data security wherein, one user with one client can't see the data of the other user with another client. It can be like client 100 in development box is for development and 110 is used for testing.

2. **User:** Input user name.

3. **Password:** Password details.

4. **Language:** Input the system language. SAP is multi lingual product.

# CHANGE SAP LOGON PASSWORD

To change the system password input the current username password at log in time and click on "New Password".

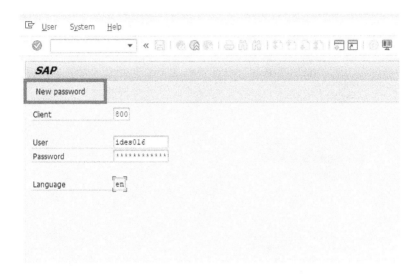

*Figure 3*

## Input new password and Hit enter.

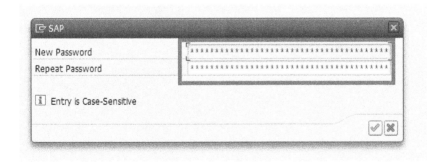

*Figure 1*

# Initial SAP Screen

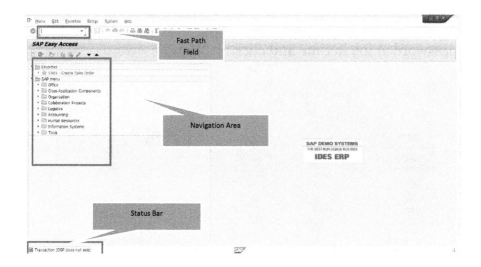

*Figure 1*

# TRANSACTION CODES

To view or maintain any data in SAP or access different business processes you need to know the corresponding transaction. Every transaction has a unique code.

## Types of transaction code

### Standard Transaction code:

SAP has standard set of transaction codes each of which has a different operation and follow for the most part, a nomenclature like 01, 02. 03 as suffixes. Like for creating a sales order its VA01, for changing a sales order it is VA02, to display, it is VA03.

### Custom Transaction Code:

Similarly, if we need to develop a custom functionality which is not available in standard then we can develop a custom program and associate a custom transaction code to it.

Custom code generally starts with 'Z', ZVA01 etc. (SAP Recommended)

Program starting with 'Y' are local (test programs) generally not transported for production system.

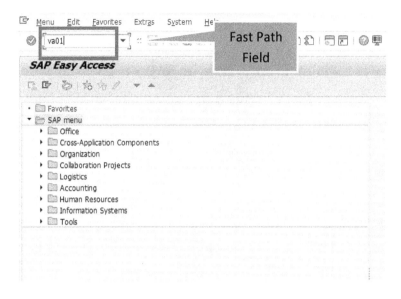

*Figure 1*

## Input the transaction code and hit Enter.

Following screen can be further used to input the details [It can include series of screens as well] and create sales order.

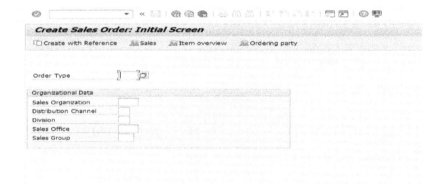

*Figure 2*

# Ways to access a transaction in SAP:

- Fast Path Field
- Favorites
- SAP Menu

## Fast Path Field

Type the Transaction Code in the Fast Path Field and press Enter on the keyboard or click the Enter icon to navigate to that transaction.

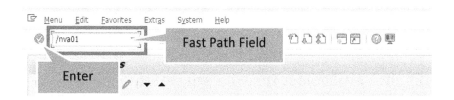

*Figure 1*

## Add Transaction Code to Favorite menu

Right click on the Favorite folder to insert most commonly used transaction code, so that you need not remember them.

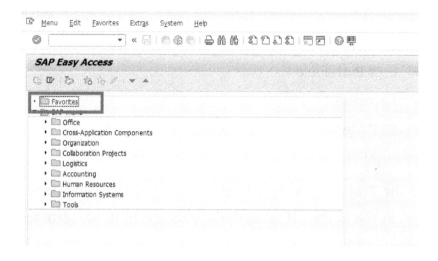

Figure 2

## Right click and select Insert transaction

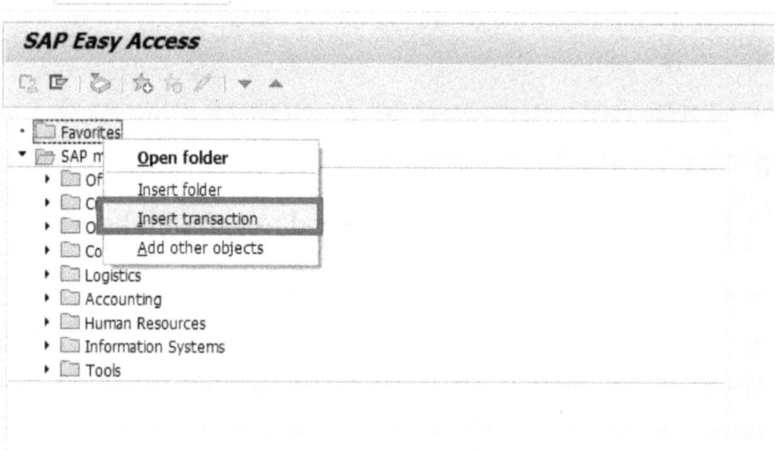

Figure 3

# Input transaction code and hit enter.

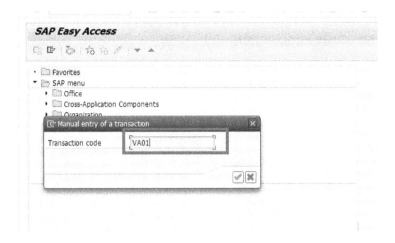

*Figure 4*

When logged in, we can double click on the desired code to access transaction.

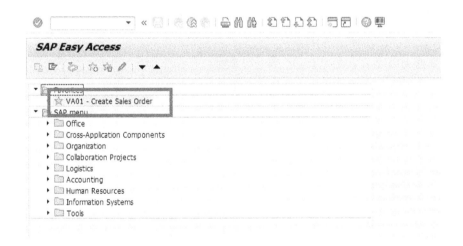

*Figure 5*

# SAP Menu

You can navigate to these transactions by double clicking on the name of the transaction

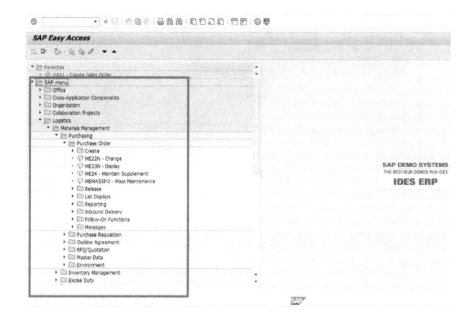

*Figure 6*

# Ending Transaction

- Select highlighted icon
- Then choose Stop Transaction

*Figure 1*

*Figure 2*

# Transaction code Details

Every transaction code is associated with a backend program which gets called when T-Code is executed. In order to see the details, input SE93 in the command box:

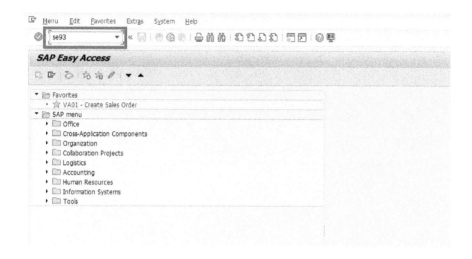

*Figure 1*

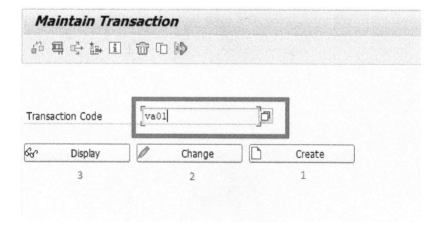

*Figure 2*

Same transaction code: SE93 is used to Create, Change & Display transaction code.

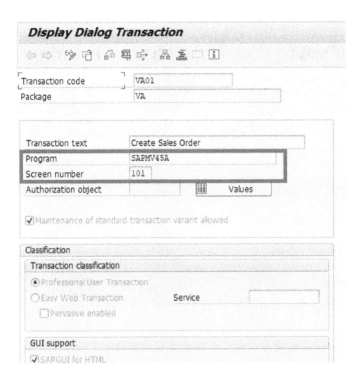

*Figure 3*

Here we can find the associated program name and screen number which will be called when a transaction code is triggered.

While creating the transaction code you need to program transaction description text which gets displayed on the title bar.

# SESSIONS

A session is like a window within SAP

- Opening up a new session allows you to work on more than one thing at the same time
- Follow: System> Create Session or Select the Create Session button from the standard toolbar
- You must have chosen the Windows GUI, not the Web GUI for this to work
- You can have up to six sessions running simultaneously

## Click on the button below to see options:

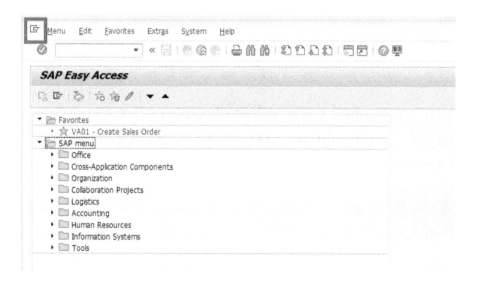

*Figure 1*

Also, you can also click on 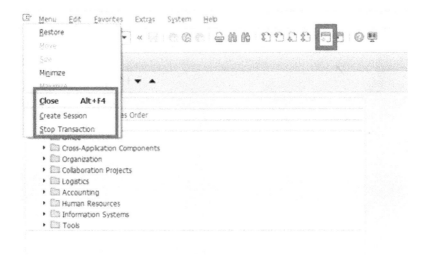 to create a new session

*Figure 2*

1) Close: It will close the current session or screen.

2) Create Session: Action will create a new session or open new window. At max, we can have 6 sessions opened in a client.

3) Stop: This action will stop the current transaction and come out to sap menu screen.

# New Session Looks Like:

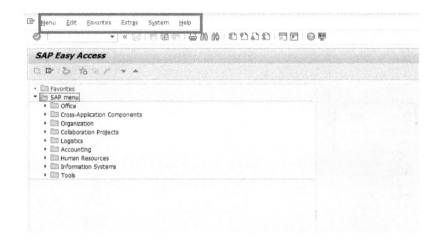

*Figure 3*

Above highlighted box is for standard menu options for Print, Save Find, and Scroll etc.

# New Session from Fast Path Field (Different Window)

- Type /O before the transaction code and hit Enter
- You will be taken directly to the new transaction in a new session without closing what you were working on
- You can do this from any screen

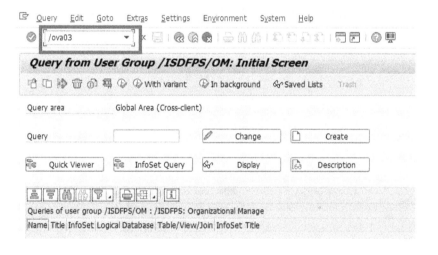

*Figure 1*

# New Session from Fast Path Field (Same Window)

- Type /N before the transaction code and hit Enter
- You will be taken directly to the new transaction in same session and current session shall be closed.

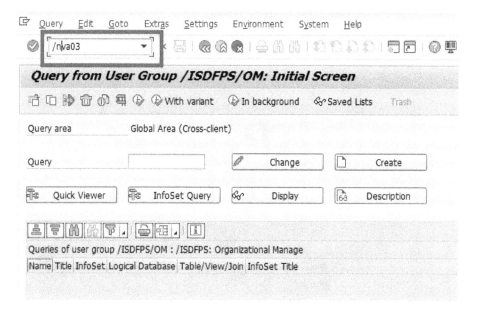

*Figure 1*

# Ending Session

## From the menu bar choose System> End Session

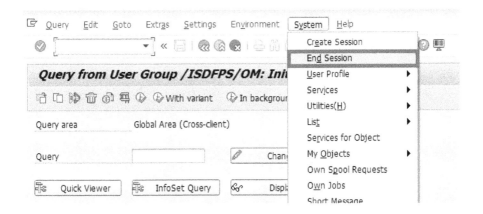

*Figure 6*

## Or click close button on top right hand corner.

*Figure 7*

# Logoff SAP

If single session is opened on screen (Only 1 window is opened)

Select yellow button at top of screen (see Fig 8)

*Figure 8*

Warning message to save data

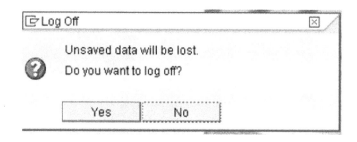

*Figure 9*

Also, you can select System->Logoff

*Figure 10*

# SAP Easy Access Menu

The SAP Easy Access Menu includes all transactions offered by SAP, grouped in folders per SAP modules (FI/CO, MM, etc.). It is not tailored to the user's specific needs

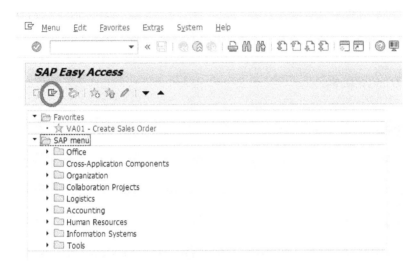

*Figure 11*

# SAP Menu Bar

The SAP Menu Bar CHANGES from one screen to another. You follow a menu path to access a function or a transaction.

*Figure 12*

# SET UP USER PROFILE

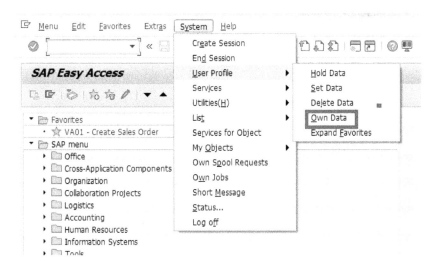

*Figure 1*

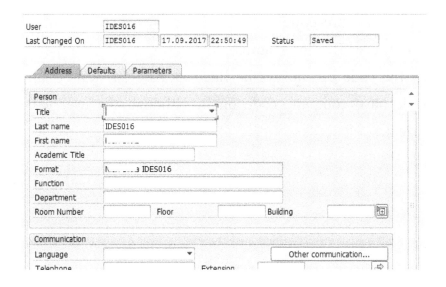

*Figure 2*

Here the user can change the Printer, decimal notation and

date formats:

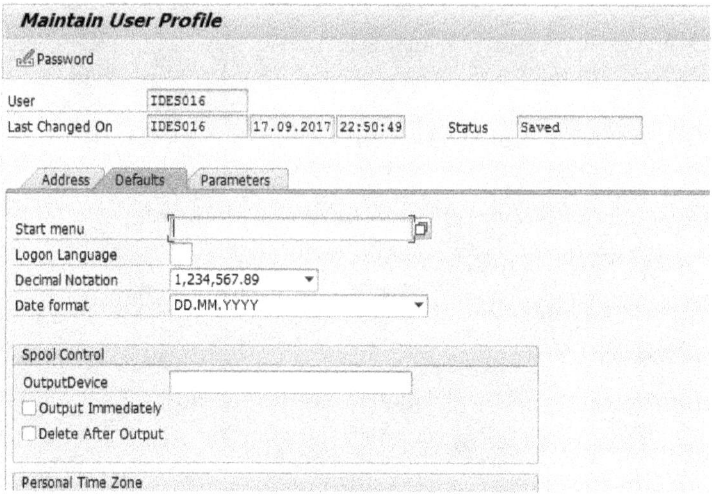

*Figure 3*

**Default Parameters:**

These are for pre-populating the screen fields with a value based on user ID. For example, for a user at ABC Company code, the code can always be filled as ABC (if transaction code is have company code on it, although the user can change it.)

Figure 4

**Parameter ID is found in the technical setting of field on screen.**

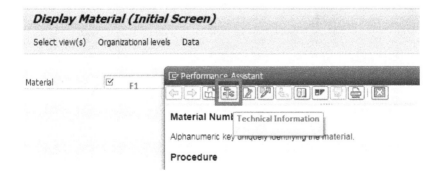

Figure 5

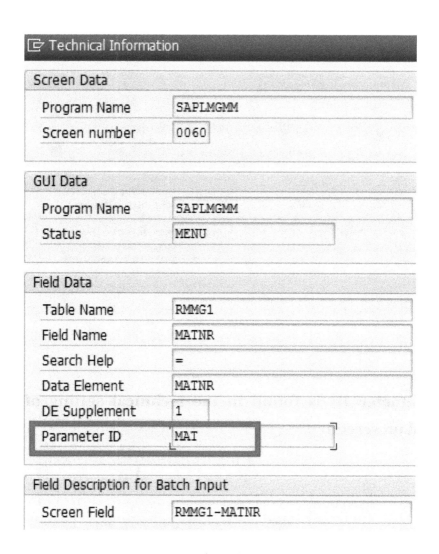

*Figure 6*

# SAP SERVICES

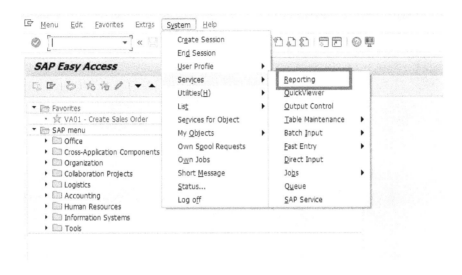

*Figure 1*

User can input the program name to execute output:

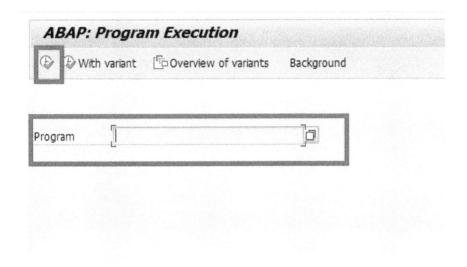

*Figure 2*

Every transaction code is associated with a program name. By calling a transaction code, ultimately the program name is called in the backend.

## Print Commands

All print commands or printing actions create spools in the system. While one has access to one's own spools all the time, to view others' spools is a matter of authorizations so we will look here how to look them up:

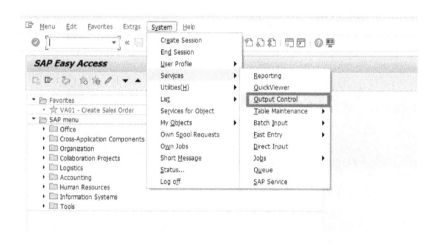

*Figure 3*

Menu option can be selected to view all the print outputs issued. All the print commands generate a spool request (having the details of the output). They can also be accessed with transaction code SP01.

Provide Filter/selection criteria e.g. date, and execute (F8)

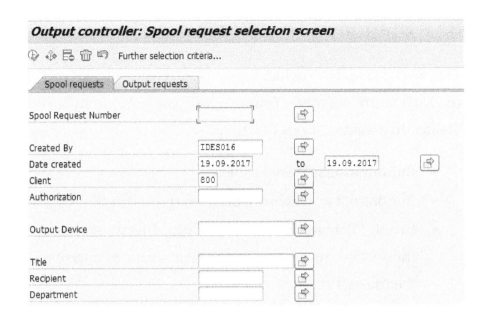

*Figure 1*

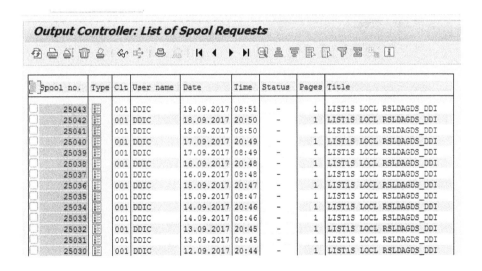

*Figure 5*

# SAP Standard Tool Bar

The SAP Standard Toolbar does NOT change from one transaction to another. You can use the SAP Standard Toolbar to execute various functions.

- Buttons available are enabled
- Buttons not available are disabled (greyed out)
- In the "Transaction Box", you can directly access a transaction, without using the SAP Menu, by entering the transaction code

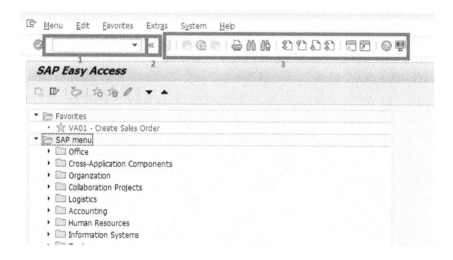

*Figure 6*

1. Transaction code box
2. Click to open and close transaction box.
3. Standard tool bar.

# Options Menu

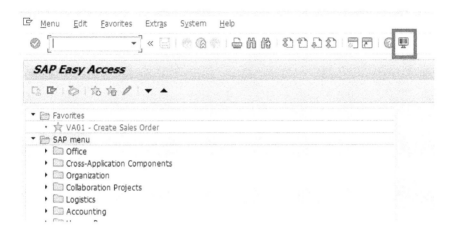

*Figure 7*

To change various display settings on screen:

*Figure 8*

Visual Design: It provides various options to changes Theme, font, color etc.

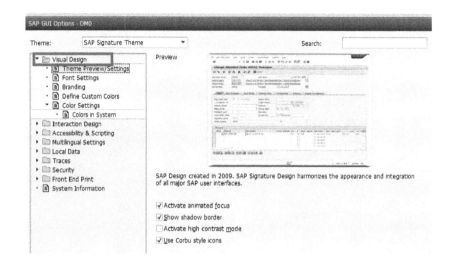

*Figure 9*

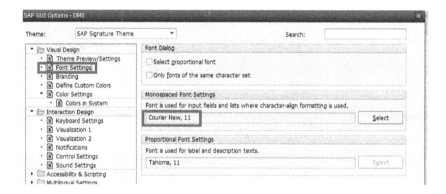

*Figure 10*

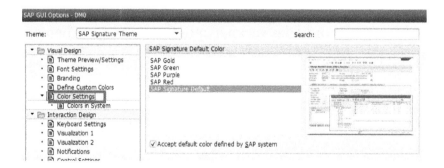

*Figure 11*

40

## Interaction Design

There are various options present under the interaction design, for keyboard shortcuts and visualization relevant options.

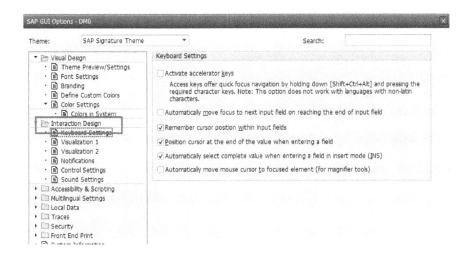

*Figure 12*

**Keyboard Setting**: Few important ones  are listed below

## Activate Accelerator Setting

It can be checked to enable various key board options:

| Hot Keys | Result |
| --- | --- |
| ALT + F12 | Calls the menu dialog box for Adjust Local Layout |
| CTRL + Shift + P | Creates a hardcopy which shows no menu dialog box and can also contain status texts and modal dialog boxes |
| CTRL + / | Cursor jumps directly to the command field. |
| CTRL + I | Cursor jumps to the first focusable field or control. |
| CTRL + + | Creates new session. |
| CTRL + ; | Creates SAP shortcut. |
| ContextMenu-Key = SHIFT + F10 | Calls context menu. |
| CTRL + Q | Shows tooltip for the focus control. |
| ESC in command field | Closes the dropdown list, if it is open. |
| CTRL + Z, CTRL + Y | Cancel and restores in input field. |
| Shift + CTRL + Alt + First Character of a Screen Element's Label | Cursor jumps from the current screen element to the next one, for which the label begins with the character, if the setting "Switch on access Keys" in Keyboard Settings is on. These screen elements include fields, checkboxes, dropdown lists, pushbuttons, and radio buttons. They exclude controls like ALV, HTML, and APOGrid. |
| CTRL + A | Selects all data in the User Interface element that is in focus (not available in all User Interface elements) |
| . | |

*Figure 13*

## Automatically move focus to next input field:

If automatic tabbing is activated, the cursor automatically moves to the next input field when the maximum number of characters has been entered in a field. This function is useful if you are entering a large amount of data and you do not want to press the TAB key to move from field to field. Auto TAB only works at the end of an input field. For example, if the *Material* field can contain 12 characters, but the material number you enter is only 7 characters long, you must still press the TAB key to move to the next input field. Visualization setting:

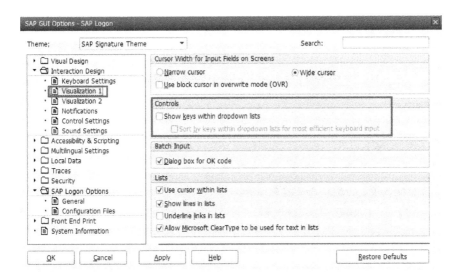

*Figure 14*

**Controls**

| Setting | Function |
|---|---|
| Show keys within dropdown lists | **Selected:** Keys are also displayed in dropdown lists. This setting is useful for experts who prefer working with keys rather than textual descriptions. **Unselected:** Only texts are displayed in dropdown lists. |
| Sort by keys within dropdown lists... | **Selected:** All items in the dropdown list are sorted by key. **Unselected:** The items are sorted in accordance with the application settings. |

*Figure 15*

43

# SAP Application Toolbar

The SAP Application Toolbar changes from one screen to another.

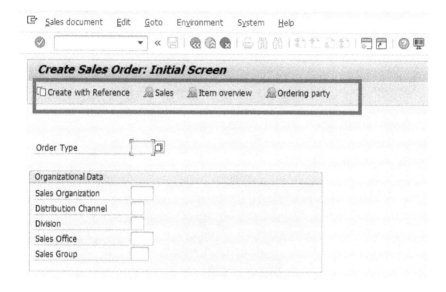

*Figure 16*

# SAP Status Bar

The SAP Status Bar does NOT change from one screen to another. It tells you WHERE you are in SAP:

- Which environment you are using (Production, Development, Quality).
- In which session, you are in (as you can open up to 6 sessions).
- Which client you are using

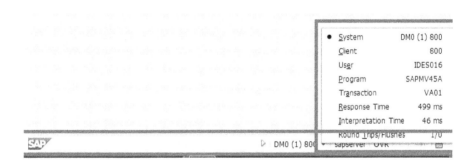

*Figure 17*

45

# SAP System Messages

There are three types of system messages:

- Error Message
- Warning Message
- Success Message

| Message Type | Code | Message Description |
|---|---|---|
| Error Messages | ⊗ | Indicates a problem that must be corrected before continuing. |
| Information Messages | ⊘ | No action is required. SAP is informing you of a particular fact or condition. However, you must hit Enter to proceed past the message. |
| Warning Messages | ① | Indicates there may be a problem with the data you have entered. You may have to correct the problem before continuing. |

*Figure 18*

46

# SAP Function Keys

Keyboard shortcuts can be used to navigate around SAP. Different transaction codes have different function keys. Right click on the screen to see the function keys.

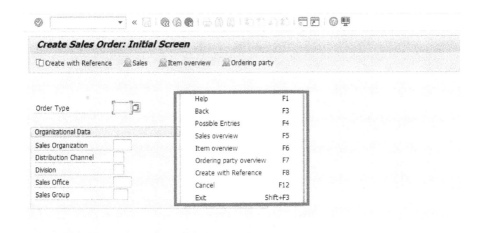

*Figure 19*

# SAP Technical Field Information/Help

If you click on input field on SAP screen, and press F1 key on the keyboard you can get to know the field description:

Click on Order Type input field and click F1

*Figure 20*

It gives you information on how to fill the specific field on screen

Clicking on Technical Information Button gives you information like program name, table name and other technical details which comes in very handy at times.

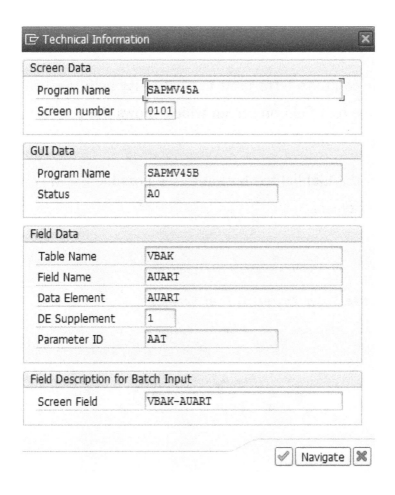

*Figure 11*

Clicking on portal button gives you access to the online SAP
Library available via the internet.

# SAP F4 help

Another common term used in SAP is F4 help. F4 help is applicable to a field on screen which shows the possible list of values for that field.

Click on the highlighted button to see possible list of values for Order type:

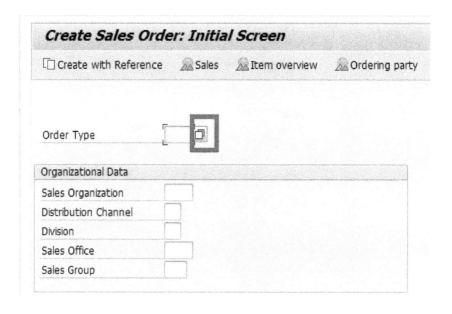

*Figure 22*

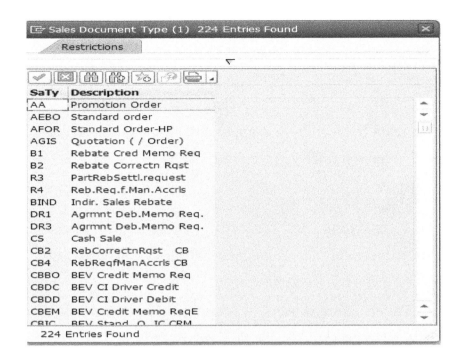

*Figure 13*

51

# VARIANTS

Strictly speaking, variants are variations of screens – both, input and output. They are not cross application components but 'common' components. Most of the screens in SAP behave similarly for the purpose of creating variants. The purpose of variants is twofold:

- To enable to user to save time by setting up screens with roughly the same data that may be needed every time the transaction is run
- To let different users who may all be using the same transaction have their differentiation from each other in terms of inputs and outputs by naming their variants as suitable to them.

Variants are best explained by an example.

# Input Variants

Let us call a standard SAP transition to look up account balances FBL3N:

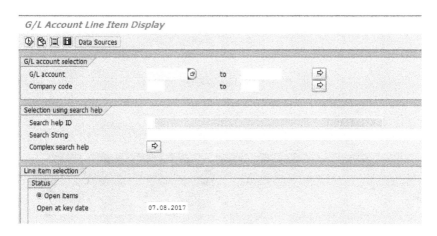

*Figure 1:* G/L Account Line Item Display

Let us assume you as an accounts person, is responsible for the company code SFE1 and for G/L accounts 100000 to 199999. A simple variant can be set up with these values:

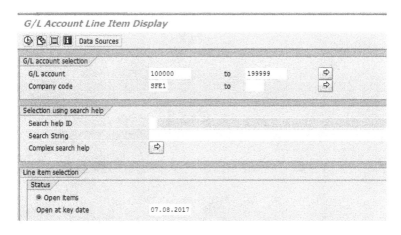

*Figure 2:* G/L Account Line Item Display

Save the values either by clicking on 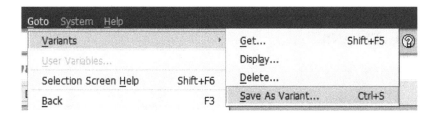 or:

*Figure 3:* Variants options

## Give it a name:

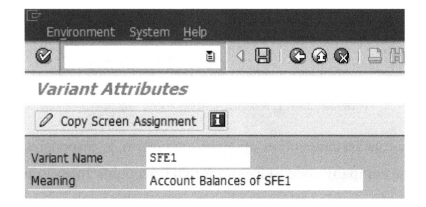

*Figure 4:* Variant Attributes

## And save it:

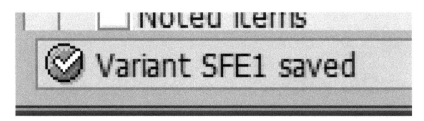

*Figure 5:* Variant Saved message

Next time when you call the transaction FBL3N simply click

on the button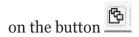

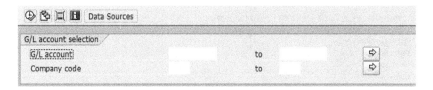

*Figure 6:* Find Variant

## And enter the name of the variant if you know it:

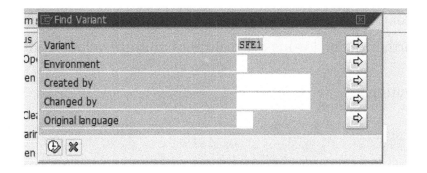

*Figure 7:* Find Variant

Or simply execute the above window to get a list of all and double click to choose the one you want:

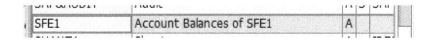

*Figure 8:* Find Variant

The figures you entered at the time of creating the variant will come on the screen so they don't have to be entered every time.

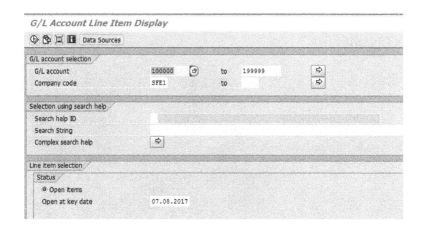

*Figure 9:* G/L Account Line Item Display

The above was a simple example of a variant. The inputs can be further defined using the feature of multiple values using

the button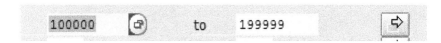

*Figure 10:* Multiple Selection

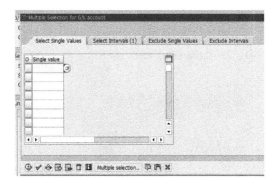

*Figure 11:* Multiple Selection

As you notice above, there are 4 tabs:

**1. Select single values** – here, G/L accounts. You can keep adding the G/Ls you want the balances for, manually or, copy them from a spreadsheet and paste them using the icon. You can also use the button to upload a text file though this is seldom used as the same objective can be achieved by a simpler copy/paste feature.

**2. Select Intervals** – this is what we have chosen in our variant:

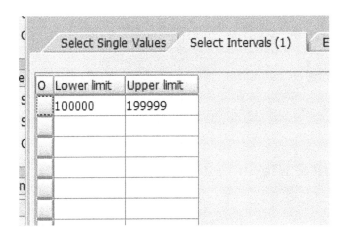

*Figure 12:* Multiple Selection

As seen above, multiple intervals of different ranges can be chosen.

**3 and 4** – Exclude single values and exclude ranges – work exactly the same way as 1 and 2 except these are for excluding the G/L accounts while 1 and 2 were for including them.

# Display Variant

Let us stay with our variant and execute the report using the button Execute:

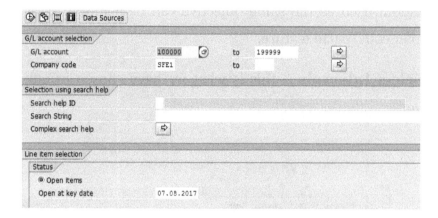

*Figure 13:* G/L Account Line Item Display

## Some kind of a layout emerges:

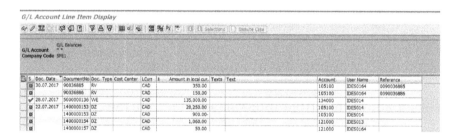

*Figure 14:* G/L Account Line Item Display

The above is the display of the report based on some parameters. Let us see what they are and how this can be customized to our requirement.

The first is how to display. As seen above, this is an Excel friendly layout. It can be changed to a more generic layout using:

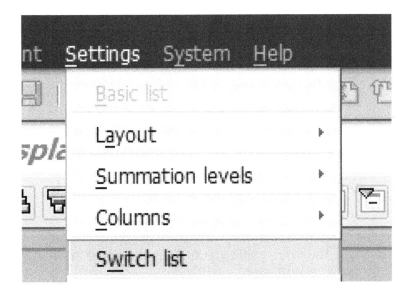

*Figure 15:* Setting options

G/L Balances
G/L Account * *
Company Code SFE1

| St | Doc. Date | DocumentNo | Type | Cost Ctr | LCurr | Amount in local cur. | Texts | Text | Account | User Name | Reference |
|---|---|---|---|---|---|---|---|---|---|---|---|
| | 30.07.2017 | 90036885 | RV | | CAD | 350.00 | | | 105100 | IDES0164 | 0090036885 |
| | 30.07.2017 | 90036886 | RV | | CAD | 150.00 | | | 105100 | IDES0164 | 0090036886 |
| | 28.07.2017 | 5000000136 | WE | | CAD | 135,000.00 | | | 134000 | IDES014 | |
| | 22.07.2017 | 1400000153 | DZ | | CAD | 20,250.00 | | | 105100 | IDES014 | |
| | 22.07.2017 | 1400000153 | DZ | | CAD | 900.00- | | | 105100 | IDES014 | |
| | 22.07.2017 | 1400000154 | DZ | | CAD | 1,060.00 | | | 121000 | IDES013 | |
| | 22.07.2017 | 1400000157 | DZ | | CAD | 50.00 | | | 121000 | IDES0164 | |
| | 22.07.2017 | 1800000226 | DR | | CAD | 1,000.00 | | | 105100 | IDES014 | |

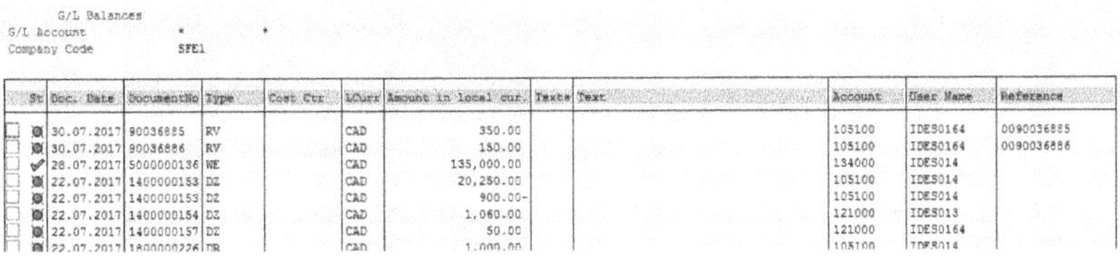

*Figure 16:* G/L Account Balances

Most people will prefer the Excel type grid so we work with that:

Identify a few of these Windows based icons and work with them:

*Figure 17:* Base Icons

The SAP specific ones,  refer to how the layouts can be created and saved:

As we notice, the columns currently available to us in this report are:

| S... | Doc. Date | DocumentNo | Doc. Type | Cost Center | LCurr | Σ | Amount in local cur. | Texts | Text | Account | User Name | Reference |
|------|-----------|------------|-----------|-------------|-------|---|----------------------|-------|------|---------|-----------|-----------|
| 20.07.2017 | 0002689S | DV | | CAD | | 250.00 | | | | 105100 | TDSS0164 | 000002689S |

*Figure 18:* Available columns

The source of these columns are SAP tables – in this case, accounting tables (next section, ideally, to be visited once you have finished the rest of this book).

If you wish to add/delete or re-arrange any of these columns, click on :

60

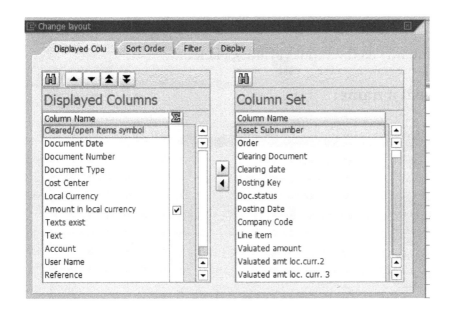

*Figure 19:* Change Layout

As you notice, the section on the left is the list of the columns displayed in the order from top to bottom > left to right in the report. The right section is the list of more fields/columns available though it is not necessary that all of them hold data. If you wish to see something new/additional or want to hide any, just double click on it and it flips from one column to the other as clicked.

The keys are useful to find, or move up or down the list.

Once you are satisfied with what you require in your report and want to save it with the idea of recalling it every time (same way as the input variant), click on  :

## Give it a name:

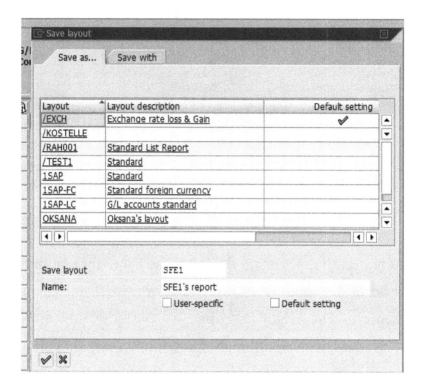

*Figure 20:* Save Layout

## You can use the buttons:

*Figure 21:* Save option

To save as specific to you OR as a default layout. It is HIGHLY recommended NOT to save as a default layout otherwise everyone will see only that as a default and will have to change it to their requirements which will not be a very useful thing for other users. So we save this as user specific:

*Figure 22:* Save Layout

*Figure 23:* Layout saved message

Next time we run this report, we can call for our display variant using the icon :

## Click on the hyperlink SFE1 as below:

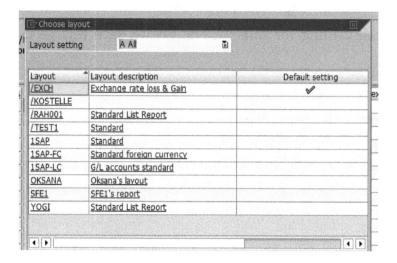

*Figure 24:* Choose Layout

## The message displayed at the bottom is:

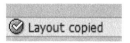

*Figure 25:* Layout copied message

This ensures whatever you had asked for in the layout SFE1 is not on the screen displayed for you.

For the most part, this variant functionality in SAP is exactly the same across all screens and all modules thereby making your life infinitely easier.

Not only do variants help you save time, they can also present you with data relating to the documents themselves e.g. by checking any particular line, you can go straight into the document and make changes for whatever is possible to be changed.

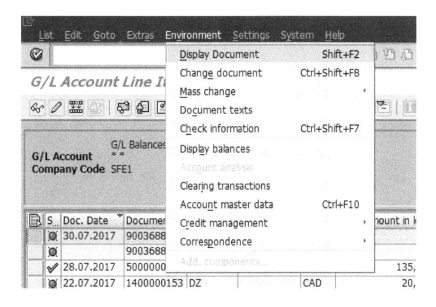

*Figure 26:* Environment options

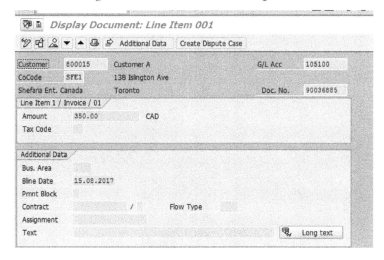

*Figure 27*

## Display Document

Lots of other data is visible through variants so you are saved the enormous amount of time in opening up different sessions to look up any transactions or documents.

# MAIN SYMBOLS

| Symbol | Meaning | Extended meaning/ Function |
|---|---|---|
| **/n** | New | Before the T-Code, replaces the existing screen with the new T-Code |
| **/o** | Another | Before the T-Code, replaces opens up a new screen with the new T-Code |
| **/nex** | Exit | When you put /nex in transaction code box then it will close all the sessions and exit. |
| ⬚ | Session key | Opens up a new session – |

| | | up to 6 can be opened simultaneously in the latest version, at the time of writing |
|---|---|---|
| | Execute button or F8 | Executes the program to give results based on what the user has selected on the input screen |
| | Navigation keys | Goes one step back (also F3), goes completely out of the transaction and cancels the current screen, respectively |
| | Page scroll | First page, previous page, |

| | | next page and last page respectively |
|---|---|---|
| 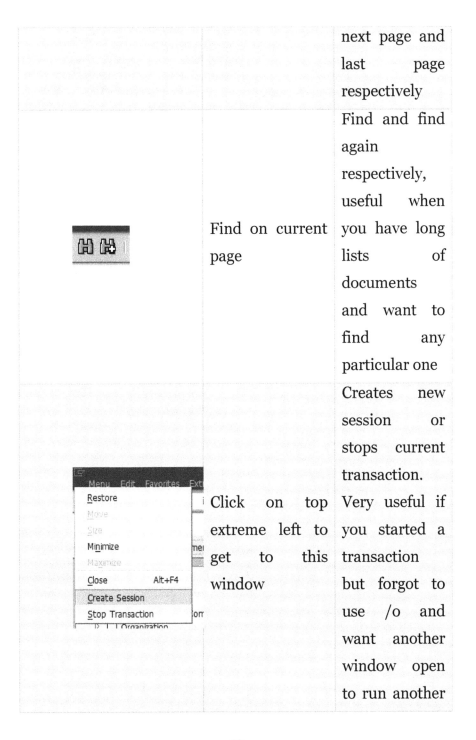 | Find on current page | Find and find again respectively, useful when you have long lists of documents and want to find any particular one |
| | Click on top extreme left to get to this window | Creates new session or stops current transaction. Very useful if you started a transaction but forgot to use /o and want another window open to run another |

| | transaction. Also useful to cancel the current transaction if you gave incorrect input parameters and it is taking too long to fetch the results. |

# SAP SPRO TRANSACTION

SPRO is the transaction to maintain the functional configurations as per client's requirements. It stands for SAP Project Reference Object

## Now, click on SAP Reference IMG

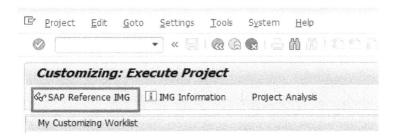

Here you can find the option to maintain functional configurations domain wise (FI, Material Management, Logistics etc.). Although, it is recommended that transaction should only be used by functional consultant for respective modules only.

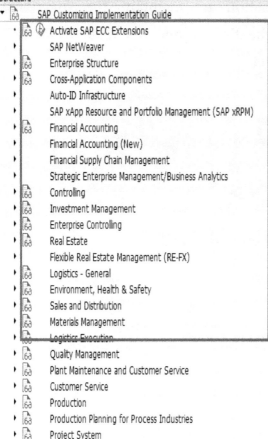

Existing BC Sets  &BC Sets for Activity  &Activated BC Sets for Activity  [i] Release Notes

Structure

▼ SAP Customizing Implementation Guide
  • Activate SAP ECC Extensions
  ▸   SAP NetWeaver
  ▸ Enterprise Structure
  ▸ Cross-Application Components
  ▸   Auto-ID Infrastructure
  ▸   SAP xApp Resource and Portfolio Management (SAP xRPM)
  ▸ Financial Accounting
  ▸   Financial Accounting (New)
  ▸   Financial Supply Chain Management
  ▸   Strategic Enterprise Management/Business Analytics
  ▸ Controlling
  ▸ Investment Management
  ▸ Enterprise Controlling
  ▸ Real Estate
  ▸   Flexible Real Estate Management (RE-FX)
  ▸ Logistics - General
  ▸ Environment, Health & Safety
  ▸ Sales and Distribution
  ▸ Materials Management
  ▸ Logistics Execution
  ▸ Quality Management
  ▸ Plant Maintenance and Customer Service
  ▸ Customer Service
  ▸ Production
  ▸ Production Planning for Process Industries
  ▸ Project System

72

# TRANSACTION CODE SE16H - DATA DISPLAY

## Transaction Code SE16H - General Data Display.

*Note: In many systems esp the older ones, the code being used is SE16N. It is essentially the same with a few lesser options; since SE16H is more advanced, it is being discussed here; it's knowledge will automatically enable you to understand SE16N yourself.*

All data in sap is stored in database tables.

## There are 2 main types of data in SAP

- **Master Data:** Master data is the core data is essential to operations in a specific business or business unit. For example Bank account number is basic master data to perform banking transactions.
- **Transactional Data:** Transactional data are information records that are generated directly derived as a result of transactions.

## Use of transaction code SE16H

SE16H can be used to quickly view statistical information based on database table. For example to get number of purchase order documents created for particular company code.

## Input transaction code SE16H in fast path field:

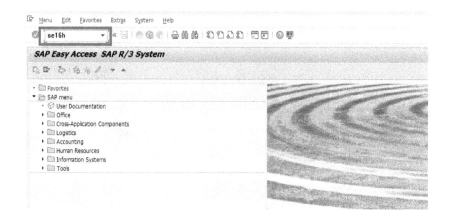

Fig 1

## Screen for General table display:

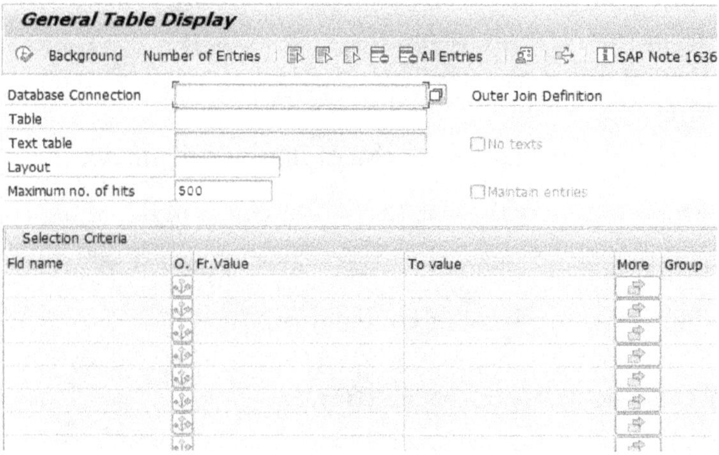

Fig 2

Now enter the table name you wish to analyze and also select checkbox for Group on the field based on which user wants to group the number of entries:

EKKO is name of database table in which Purchase order header information is stored.

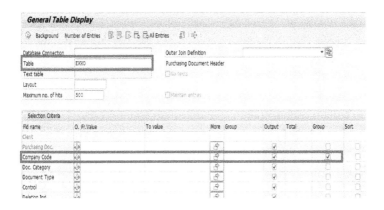

Fig 3

Click on execute button or press F8

General Table Display

Fig 4
75

**Output**:

Here you get number of purchase orders posted in the system grouped on company code field.

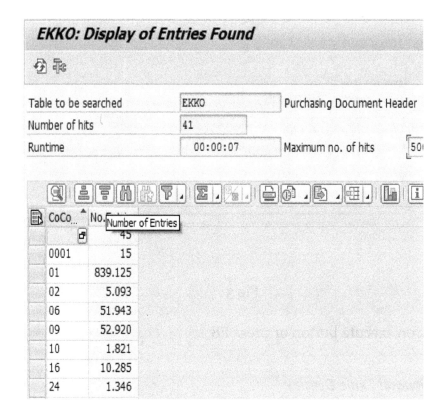

Fig 5

Similarly if the user wants to group the number of purchase orders based on Document category:

Fig 6

**Output**:

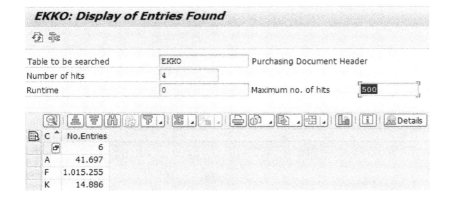

Fig 7

# SAP QUERY

## Overview:

SAP Query is used to create reports for users who have little knowledge about SAP Table data storage structure. SAP Query allows evaluating data in the SAP system.

SAP Query offers users a broad range of ways to define reporting programs and create different types of reports such as basic lists, statistics, and ranked lists.

## Features:

Following are the major components which are associated with SAP Query:

- **Info Sets** – Are base for the Query and it contains one or more database table details
- **Queries** – For the User to create and generate the Query
- **User Group** – To restrict set of Users for a specific Query plus for Authorizations
- **Quick Viewer** – A simple tool for quick report generation

# Creation:

**Step 1**: Creation of User Group – SQ03

**Step 2**: Creation of Infoset – SQ02

**Step 3**: Creation of Query – SQ01

## SAP Query – User Group Creation:

Transaction Code: SQ03

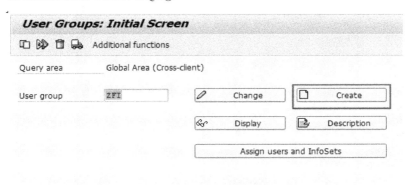

Fig 1

Create a logical set of User Group to which the InfoSet Queries would be assigned.

**SAP Query** – Info Set Creation – TABLE JOIN:

SAP database have several numbers of tables in which the transactions, master data gets stored and it's practically not feasible to have all such fields for selection when creating a query. Hence before the start of creating a query, InfoSet creation is required.

It allows selecting Fields from either the tables selected or the logical database used to get display/select in the output.

## Transaction Code: SQ02

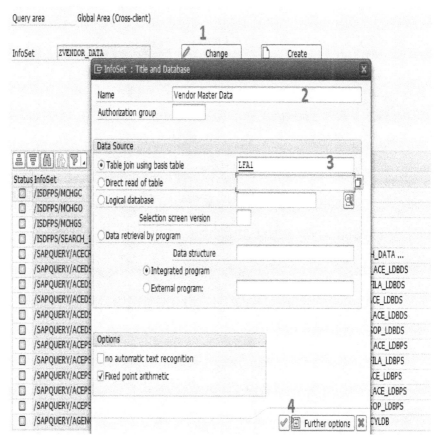

Fig 2

The InfoSet creation can be made with the Combination of Tables (Table Join), Direct read from a Single Table or with the help of Logical Database.

Click on highlighted button to add more tables to infoset

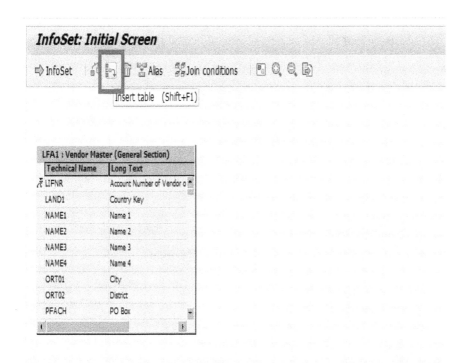

Fig 3

Click on the Infoset button and select "Include all fields"

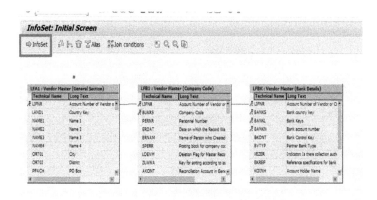

Fig 4

Field Group contains the Fields which are required either to get in the report output or in the selection screen.

Drag the Fields for the "Data Fields" to the relevant Field Groups to appear in the report.

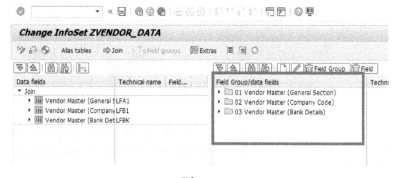

Fig 5

Once the InfoSet is created, it needs to be generated by click on "Generation" icon.

*Any changes made to the InfoSet, it needs to be re-generated every time.*

SAP Query – Assigning to User Group:

## Transaction Code: SQ03

All the InfoSet queries which are created to be assigned to one or more user group

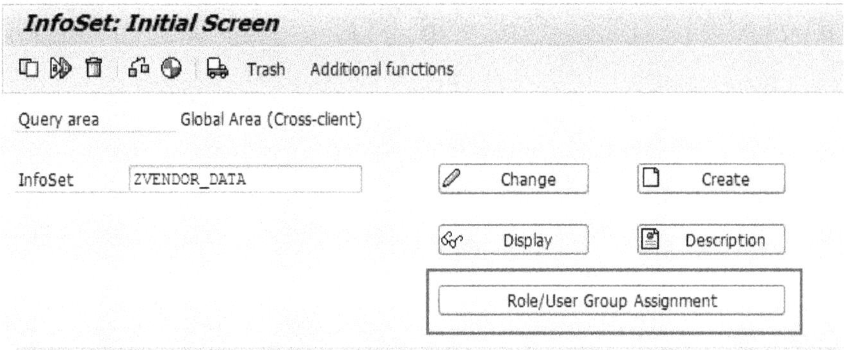

Fig 6

**InfoSet ZVENDOR_DATA: Role Assignment**

InfoSet roles and user groups ZVENDOR_DATA

| Assigned table | User group | User group name | Role |
|---|---|---|---|
| ☐ | BT | Query Course: Trainer | |
| ☐ | ERC_RECR | E-Recruiting: Recruiter | |
| ☐ | ERC_RECR_OIP | E-Recruiting: Op. InfoProvider | |
| ☐ | GPA_USER | Global Performance Analysis | |
| ☐ | HR_DE | Payroll for Germany | |
| ☐ | INGO | . | |
| ☐ | INGOWBO | . | |
| ☐ | ISU02 | Evaluation of Utilities Master | |
| ☐ | J_3RPBU18UG | PBU-18 Russia | |
| ☐ | MIRO | Logistics Invoice Verification | |
| ☐ | QDEMO | Demo-User Group | |
| ☐ | REFX | Flexible Real Estate Managemen | |
| ☐ | TESTQUERY | Test, Query delivery | |
| ☐ | WAO_46C_PT | WAO_46C_PersTimeEval_HR | |
| ☐ | WASTE | Waste Sheet: User Group | |
| ☐ | WRF_PPW | Price Planning Workbench | |
| ☐ | WTY_OR | WTY Online Reporting | |
| ☑ | ZFI | FI Users | |

Fig 7

Click on Save button for the assignment.

**SAP Query – Query Creation:**

**Transaction Code: SQ01**

Once the InfoSets are created and assigned to User Group, Query needs to be designed. It is basically known as Query Painter in which we design basic lists in WYSIWYG mode (what-you-see-is-what-you-get).

We need to select the User Group first in which query needs to be designed. Click on ⎘ icon to select the user group.

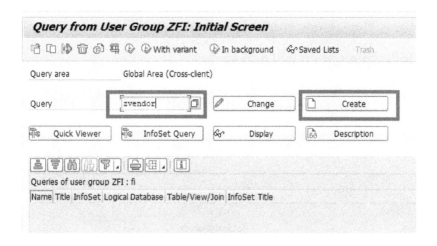

Fig 8

Now select infoset based on which report needs to be generated

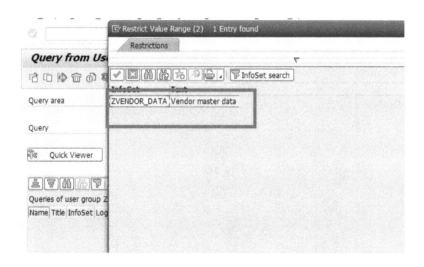

Fig 9

The following screen will appear:

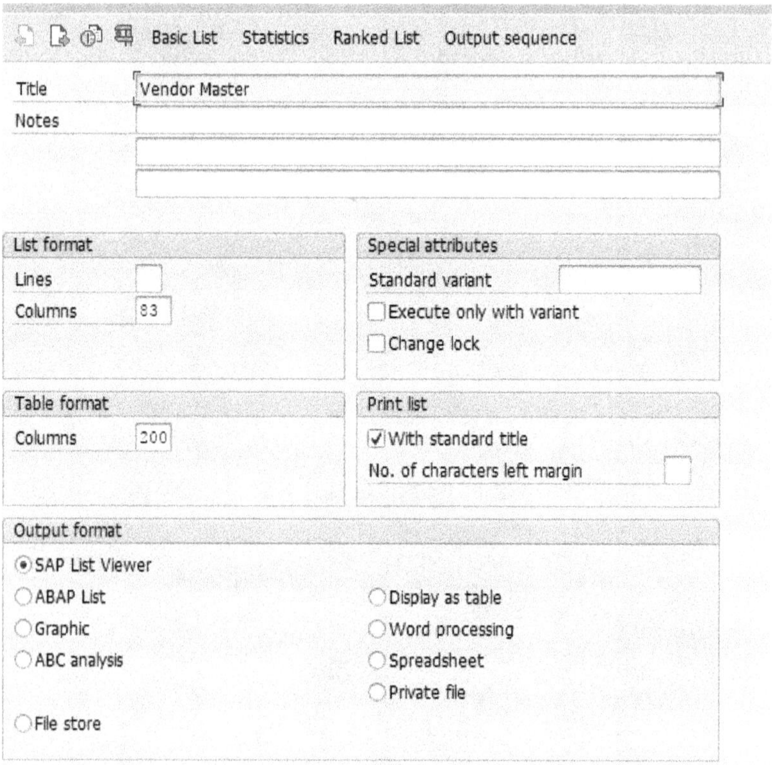

| | | Basic List | Statistics | Ranked List | Output sequence |

| Title | Vendor Master |
| Notes | |

**List format**

| Lines | |
| Columns | 83 |

**Special attributes**

| Standard variant | |
| ☐ Execute only with variant | |
| ☐ Change lock | |

**Table format**

| Columns | 200 |

**Print list**

| ☑ With standard title | |
| No. of characters left margin | |

**Output format**

⦿ SAP List Viewer
◯ ABAP List
◯ Graphic
◯ ABC analysis

◯ File store

◯ Display as table
◯ Word processing
◯ Spreadsheet
◯ Private file

Fig 10

Now, select next to select database tables from infoset

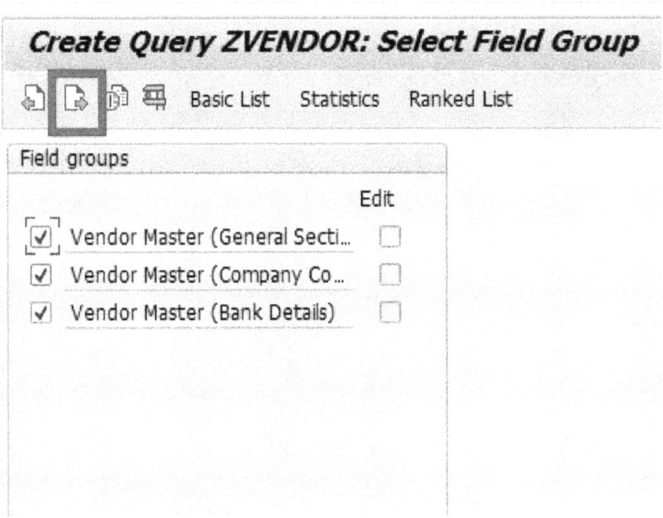

Fig 11

Now select field to be displayed in output

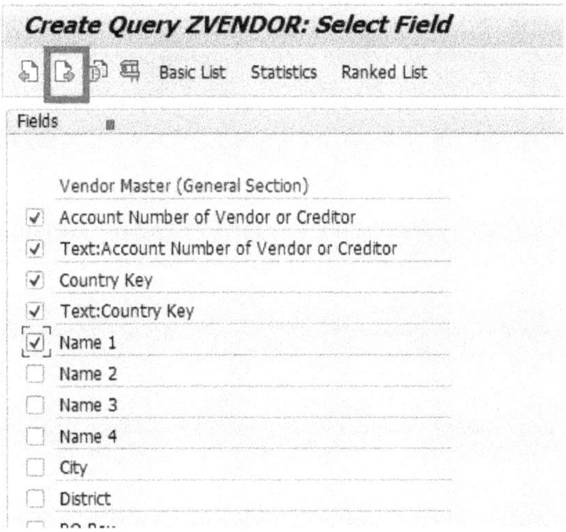

Fig 12

Now select selection fields that you desire to become a part of your selection:

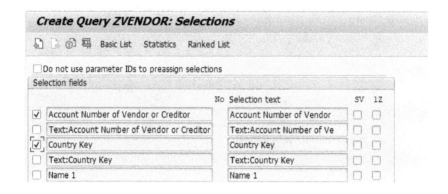

Fig 13

## Select Basic list and hit Save

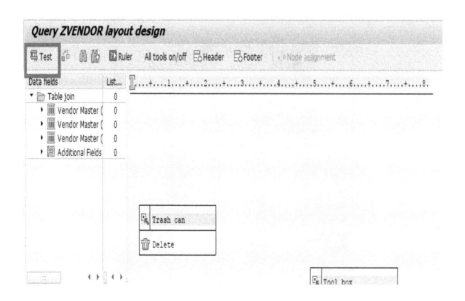

Fig 14

# Now select selection and outfields for report

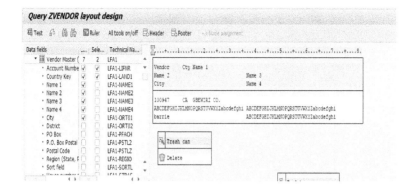

Fig 15

## Selection screen

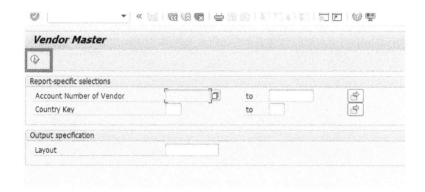

Fig 16

Output

| Vendor | Cty | Name 1 | Name 2 | Name 3 | City | Name 4 |
|---|---|---|---|---|---|---|
| 100969 | CA | Furiture | | | Schomberg | |
| 10000005 | JO | jordanian company for consultation | | | amman | |
| K0001 | JO | Jbarah industrial compay | Jbarah industrial compay | | 11941 - Jubaiha | |
| 100803 | GB | Kush | | | | |
| Z00000100 | JO | Ramsey & Sons | | | | |
| 100826 | DE | asan | | | | |
| 100838 | CA | Wood vendor for SFE1 | | | Oakville | |
| 500054 | CA | SS Vendor 2 | | | | |
| 100793 | US | | | | Mosar | |
| Z94678676 | DE | Joy limited | EDO STATE | | | |
| 100886 | PE | ANA | | | | |
| 71800 | CA | WCB - Alberta | | | Edmonton | |
| 71801 | CA | WCB - British Columbia | | | Victoria | |
| 71802 | CA | WCB - Manitoba | | | Winnipeg | |
| 71803 | CA | WCB - New Brunswick | | | Moncton | |
| 71804 | CA | WCB - Newfoundland | | | St. John's | |
| T-K500C24 | DE | H.A.G. Potsdam Gr.24 | | | Potsdam | |
| T-K500C24 | DE | H.A.G. Potsdam Gr.24 | | | Potsdam | |
| T-K500C25 | DE | H.A.G. Potsdam Gr.25 | | | Potsdam | |

**Vendor Master**

Fig 17

# SQVI QUERY (QUICKVIEWER)

All the master and transactional data in SAP is stored in database tables. We can use transaction code SQVI to view the reports based on the stored data.

The reported generated by transaction code SQVI is specific to user. It means that SQVI reports are not sharable between users.

Enter transaction code in the fast path field and hit enter.

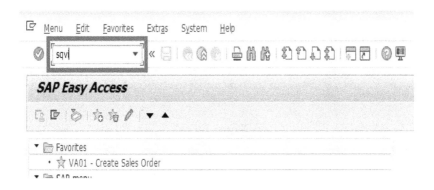

Fig 1

Transaction code can be used to Create/Change/Display the Quick view report.

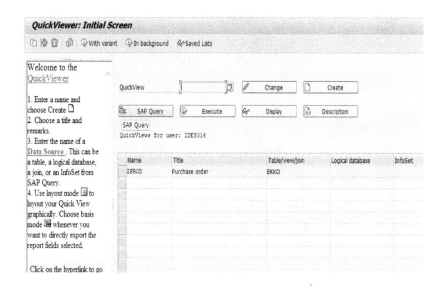

Fig 2

Enter name in the field after quick view above and click on create.

Provide details in following fields on this screen:

**Title**: Provide title of the report

Data source: It has following options in the list box.

- **Table** – If report output should be from single database table.

- **Table Join** – if report output is expected from more than 1 table. Here we can specify table or multiple tables (linked together with common key field/s) to extract report output

- **LDB**: Logical database is a group of tables related to each other. If you want to create query in HR module or complex queries in FI or SD then it is recommended to use LDB as SAP has pre-connected and optimized these table for use in the LDB

- **Infoset**: Are base for the Query and it contains one or more database table details. It can be created in transaction code SQ02.

Fig 3

Here in the above screenshot we have selected database table EKKO (database table which stores purchase order header

93

information).

Click Enter.

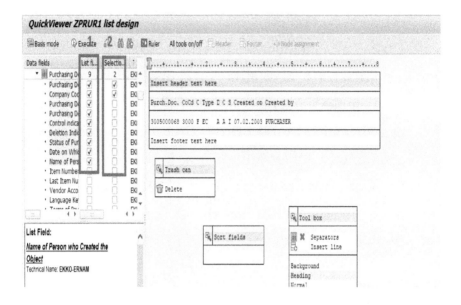

Fig 4

Here in the above screenshot:

1. Select all fields which are to be displayed in output.

2. Select the fields which are supposed to be as a part of selection criteria i.e. the fields based on which records shall be filtered and displayed.

# Execute

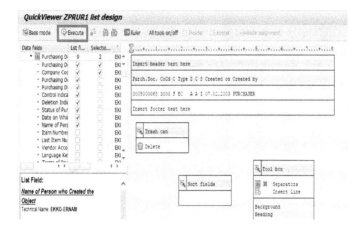

Fig 5

# Selection Screen

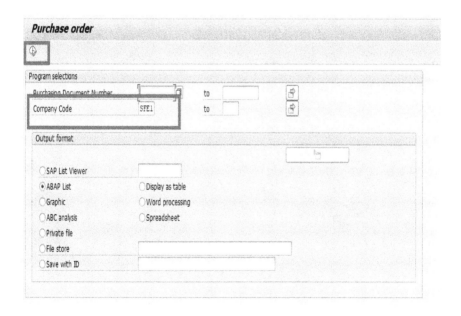

Fig 6

# Click F8 or execute button

## Purchase order

🔍 📄 📄 🔲 ⊞ ⊞ALV  📊 📤 📝 🔲 ⊞ABC  Selections

| CoCd | Purch.Doc. | C | Type | C | D | Created on | S | Created by | ItInt | LItem | Vendor |
|------|------------|---|------|---|---|-----------|---|-----------|-------|-------|--------|
| SFE1 | 4030000843 | F | NB | | | 22.01.2017 | 9 | IDES0164 | 00010 | 00010 | 100930 |
| SFE1 | 4030000844 | F | NB | | | 29.01.2017 | 9 | IDES0164 | 00010 | 00010 | 100927 |
| SFE1 | 4030000845 | F | NB | | | 29.01.2017 | 9 | IDES0164 | 00010 | 00010 | 100927 |
| SFE1 | 4030000846 | F | NB | | | 26.02.2017 | 9 | IDES0164 | 00010 | 00010 | 100838 |
| SFE1 | 4500017971 | F | FO | | | 02.03.2017 | 9 | IDES0164 | 00010 | 00010 | 100838 |
| SFE1 | 4500017972 | F | FO | | | 02.03.2017 | 9 | IDES0164 | 00010 | 00010 | 100961 |
| SFE1 | 4500017973 | F | FO | | | 02.03.2017 | 9 | IDES0164 | 00010 | 00010 | 100961 |
| SFE1 | 4500017974 | F | FO | | | 04.03.2017 | 9 | IDES0164 | 00010 | 00010 | 100961 |
| SFE1 | 4500017975 | F | FO | | | 04.03.2017 | 9 | IDES0164 | 00010 | 00010 | 100961 |
| SFE1 | 4500017976 | F | FO | | | 04.03.2017 | 9 | IDES020 | 00010 | 00010 | 100961 |
| SFE1 | 4500017977 | F | FO | | | 04.03.2017 | 9 | IDES018 | 00010 | 00010 | 100961 |
| SFE1 | 4500017978 | F | FO | | | 04.03.2017 | 9 | IDES020 | 00010 | 00010 | 100961 |
| SFE1 | 4030000847 | F | NB | | | 04.03.2017 | 9 | IDES0164 | 00010 | 00010 | 100838 |
| SFE1 | 4030000849 | F | NB | | | 04.03.2017 | 9 | IDES0164 | 00010 | 00010 | 100838 |
| SFE1 | 4030000850 | F | NB | | | 04.03.2017 | 9 | IDES0164 | 00010 | 00010 | 100838 |
| SFE1 | 4030000851 | F | NB | | | 04.03.2017 | 9 | IDES020 | 00010 | 00010 | 100953 |
| SFE1 | 4030000852 | F | NB | | | 05.03.2017 | 9 | IDES0164 | 00010 | 00010 | 100941 |
| SFE1 | 4030000853 | F | NB | | | 06.03.2017 | 9 | IDES0164 | 00010 | 00010 | 100944 |
| SFE1 | 4030000854 | F | NB | | | 06.03.2017 | 9 | IDES0164 | 00010 | 00010 | 100948 |
| SFE1 | 4030000855 | F | NB | | | 06.03.2017 | 9 | IDES0164 | 00010 | 00020 | 100952 |
| SFE1 | 4030000856 | F | NB | | | 06.03.2017 | 9 | IDES0164 | 00010 | 00010 | 100952 |

Fig 7

# TRANSFORM SQVI INTO SQ01

QuickView (SQVI) reports are fast to deploy but are user specific and not transportable. It means the following:

- It cannot be shared between users
- It needs to be created in the required system meaning it is not transportable, ideally all the development/configuration objects are created in the development system transported to quality system for process testing and eventually moved to production. However, as it can't be transported, we have to manually create Quick View report in all the systems.

In order to overcome these shortcomings we need to move QuickView query to SQ01 query (which has separately defined Infoset and Query details) – this saves a lot of time and can be shared across everyone who has access to SQ01.

Transaction Code: SQVI

As described in the section of SQVI, have created a QuickView report ZPROD to see purchase order details.

Fig 1

Now, to convert QuickView report to SQ01 query, first define the user group to which we want to assign the query.

## Transaction Code: SQ03

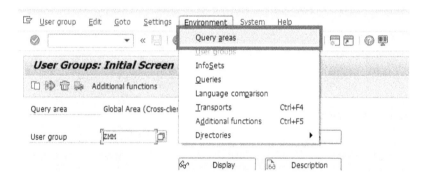

Fig 2

Select query area as standard. Standard area is specific to client (SAP Client); if required in another client also, then either it has to be transported or created again.

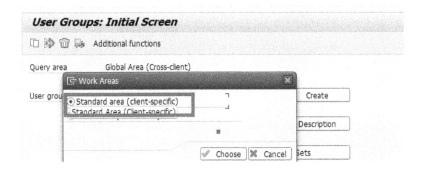

Fig 3

Input name of user group as ZMM and select create

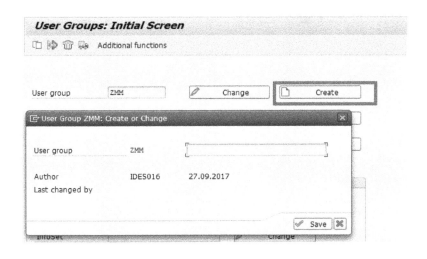

Fig 4

Here provide the description for user group and hit save.

Fig 5

User group is created

Here when you get into transaction SQ01 user group shall automatically be selected to ZMM. If it needs to be changed, then the user can go to SQ03 and select the required user group.

Transaction code SQ01

Fig 6

Here provide name of QuickView Report for which SQ01 query needs to be created

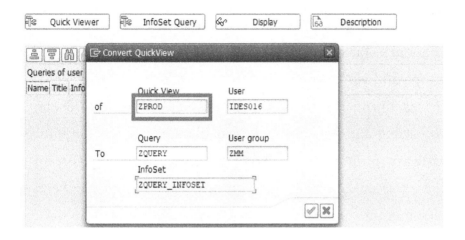

Fig 7

Also provide name of SQ01 query and infoset to be created.

Hit Enter.

☑ Query ZQUERY created

# ABOUT THE AUTHOR

Yogi Kalra has worked in the SAP field for over 25 years across multitudes of industries and with big 4 consulting experience. Based in Canada, he has done projects all over Europe and North America. Prior to entering the SAP space, he was in Business handling Sales, Distribution, Depots, Purchasing and Accounting across Chemicals and Computer hardware industries for over 12 years. He is a MBA in Finance from University of Toronto, Canada and has been instrumental in training clients during and after SAP implementations in most of the SAP modules including but not limited to, FI, MM, SD, PP and QM. This book is the first in the series of SAP books in configuration and user training in all these modules.

www.ingramcontent.com/pod-product-compliance
Lightning Source LLC
Chambersburg PA
CBHW071007050326
40689CB00014B/3525